Theory Paper Grade 5 2012 A
Model Answers

1 (a) (i) (5)

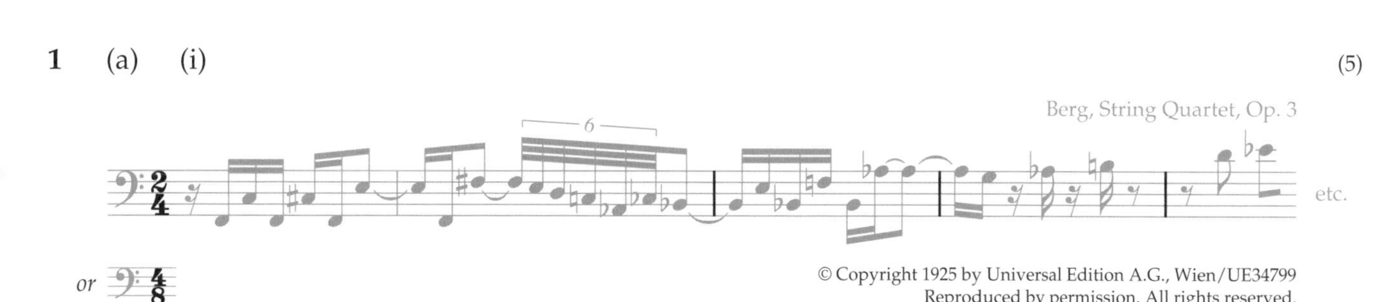

(ii) four / four demisemiquavers / two semiquavers / one quaver / four 32nd notes / two 16th notes / one eighth note (2)

(b) (i) (4)

(ii) hold the note for its full value / slight emphasis / held (2)

(iii) (2)

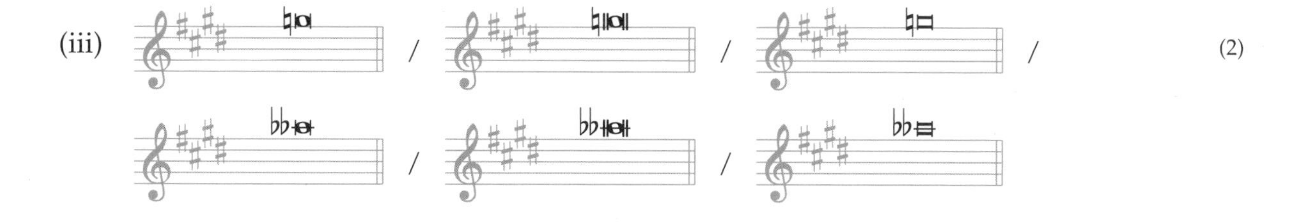

2 (10)

1 minor 6th
2 diminished octave / diminished 8th / diminished 8ve
3 major 3rd
4 augmented 4th
5 minor 10th / compound minor 3rd

3 (10)

4 (a) (i) at a walking pace in a singing style / medium speed in a singing style (4)

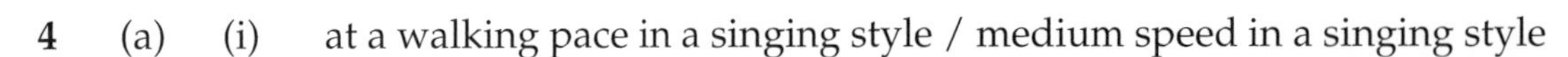

(ii) (2)

(iii) (4)

(b) (i) Chord **A** Ib Chord **B** IIb (4)

(ii) (2)

Ic – V

or $\begin{smallmatrix}6\\4\end{smallmatrix}$ – $\begin{smallmatrix}5\\3\end{smallmatrix}$

(iii) X leading note (2)

Y submediant (2)

(c) (i) G minor (2)

(ii) String violin / viola / cello / harp (2)

Woodwind flute / oboe / clarinet / cor anglais (2)

(iii) Definite pitch timpani / kettledrums / xylophone / marimba / glockenspiel / vibraphone / celesta / tubular bells (2)

Indefinite pitch side drum / snare drum / bass drum / cymbals / triangle / tambourine / castanets / tam-tam (2)

5 (10)

(a)

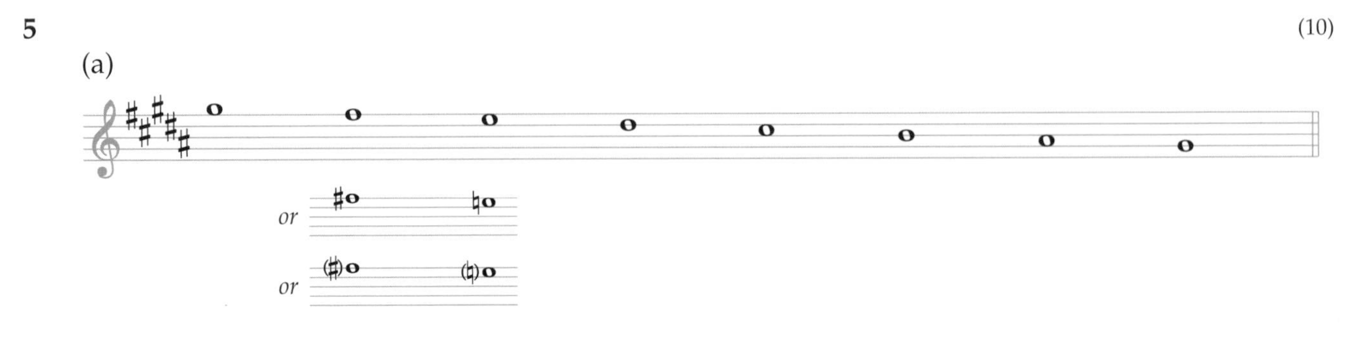

(b)

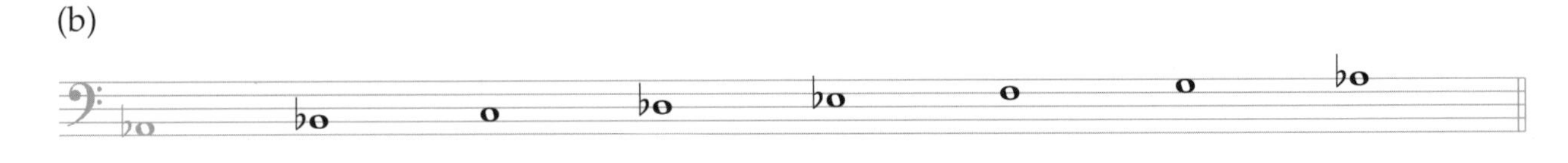

Grade
5

Music Theory Past Papers 2012 Model Answers

Music Theory Past Papers 2012
Model Answers

ABRSM Grade 5

Welcome to ABRSM's *Music Theory Past Papers 2012 Model Answers*, Grade 5. These answers are a useful resource for pupils and teachers preparing for ABRSM theory exams and should be used alongside the relevant published theory past papers.

All the answers in this booklet would receive full marks but not all possible answers have been included for practicable reasons. In these cases other reasonable alternatives may also be awarded full marks. For composition-style questions (where candidates must complete a rhythm, compose a melody based on a given opening or set text to music) only one example of the many possible answers is given.

For more information on how theory papers are marked and some general advice on taking theory exams, please refer to the booklet *These Music Exams* by Clara Taylor, which is available free of charge and can be downloaded from www.abrsm.org.

Using these answers

- Answers are given in the same order and, where possible, in the same layout as in the exam papers, making it easy to match answer to question.

- Where it is necessary to show the answer on a stave, the original stave is printed in grey with the answer shown in black, for example:

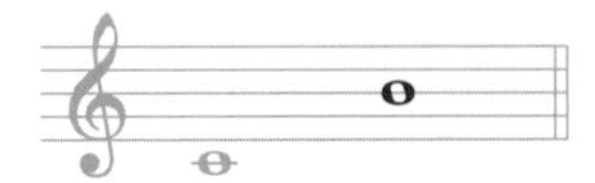

- Alternative answers are separated by an oblique stroke (/) or by *or*, for example:

getting slower / gradually getting slower

- Answers that require the candidate to write out a scale or chord have been shown at one octave only. Reasonable alternatives at different octaves can also receive full marks.

Published by ABRSM (Publishing) Ltd, a wholly owned subsidiary of ABRSM
Cover by Kate Benjamin & Andy Potts
Printed in England by Page Bros (Norwich) Ltd
Reprinted in 2014

6 *There are many ways of completing this question. Either of the specimen completions below would receive full marks.* (15)

EITHER

(a) violin

OR

(b)

7 **EITHER** (10)

(a) Chord A IV / B♭ major
Chord B V / C major
Chord C II / G minor
Chord D V / C major
Chord E I / F major

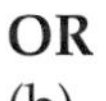

OR

(b)

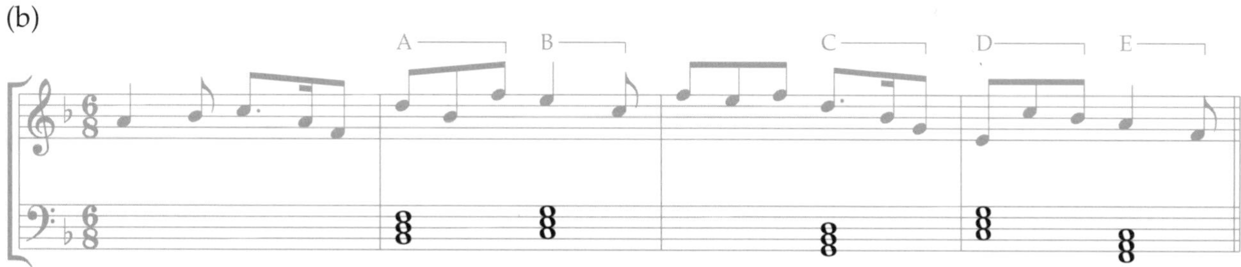

Theory Paper Grade 5 2012 B
Model Answers

1 (a) (3)

(b) (i) Chord **A** IV root / IVa (2)

Chord **B** II 3rd / IIb (2)

(ii) Bar 1 appoggiatura / leaning note (2)

Bar 3 turn / upper turn (2)

(iii) **X** mediant (2)

Y supertonic (2)

2 (10)

S

A

T

B

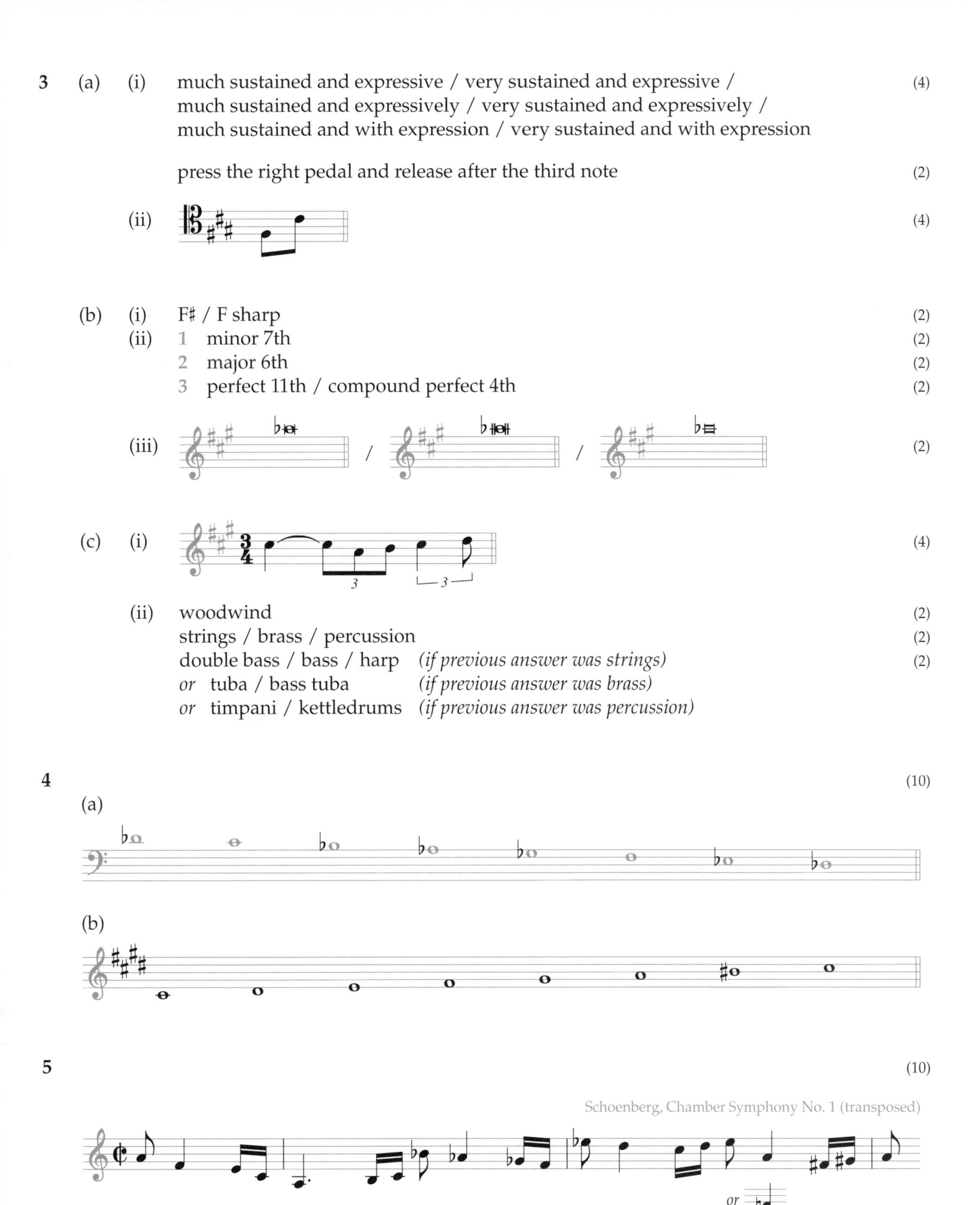
3 (a) (i) much sustained and expressive / very sustained and expressive / much sustained and expressively / very sustained and expressively / much sustained and with expression / very sustained and with expression (4)
press the right pedal and release after the third note (2)
(ii) (4)
(b) (i) F♯ / F sharp (2)
(ii) 1 minor 7th (2)
2 major 6th (2)
3 perfect 11th / compound perfect 4th (2)
(iii) / / (2)
(c) (i) (4)
3
3
(ii) woodwind (2)
strings / brass / percussion (2)
double bass / bass / harp (if previous answer was strings) (2)
or tuba / bass tuba (if previous answer was brass)
or timpani / kettledrums (if previous answer was percussion)
4 (10)
(a)
(b)
5 (10)
Schoenberg, Chamber Symphony No. 1 (transposed)
or
or

6 *There are many ways of completing this question. Either of the specimen completions below would receive full marks.* (15)

EITHER

(a) cello

OR

(b)

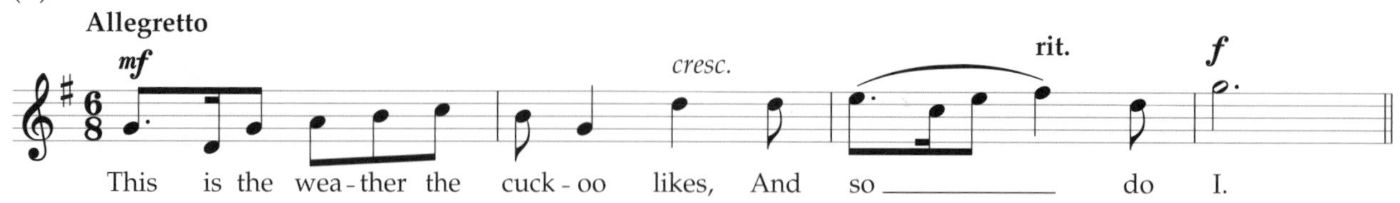

7 EITHER (10)

(a) Chord A IV / C major
Chord B V / D major
Chord C I / G major
Chord D IV / C major
Chord E I / G major

OR

(b)

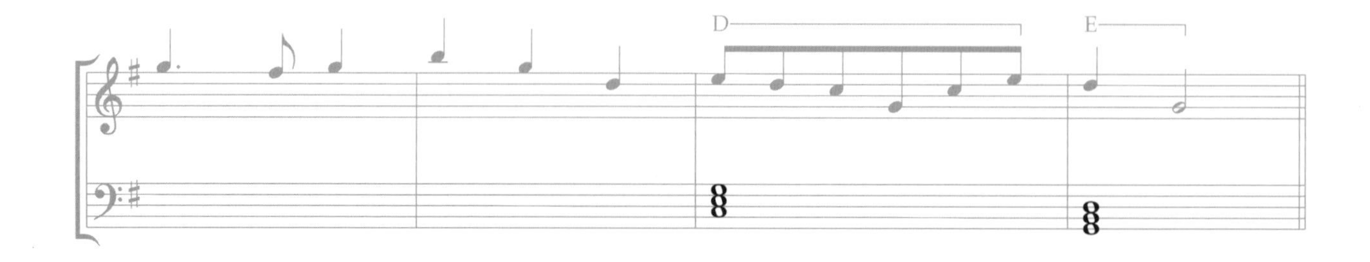

Theory Paper Grade 5 2012 C
Model Answers

1 (a) Bar 1: 7/8 Bar 3: 6/8 Bar 4: 9/8 (6)

(b) (i) Chord X V root / Va (2)
Chord Y IV 3rd / IVb (2)
Chord Z I 5th / Ic (2)

(ii) (3)

2
1 major 10th / compound major 3rd (10)
2 augmented 4th
3 minor 7th
4 diminished octave / diminished 8th / diminished 8ve
5 perfect 5th

3 (10)

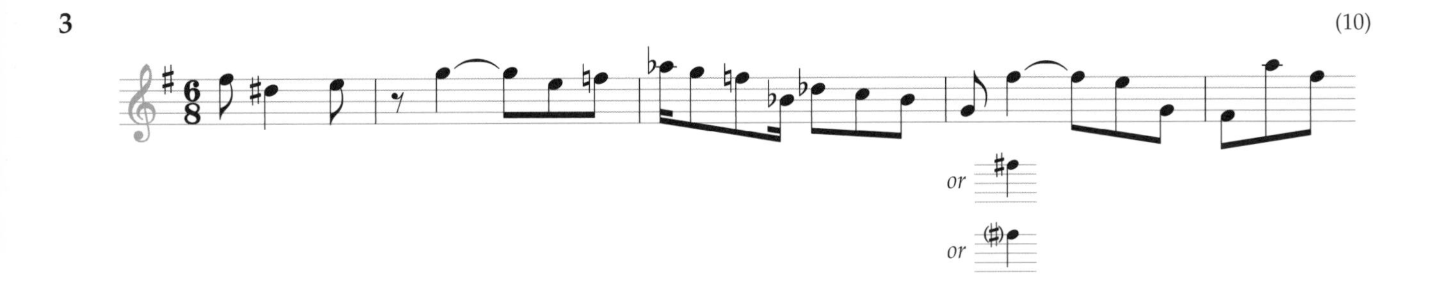

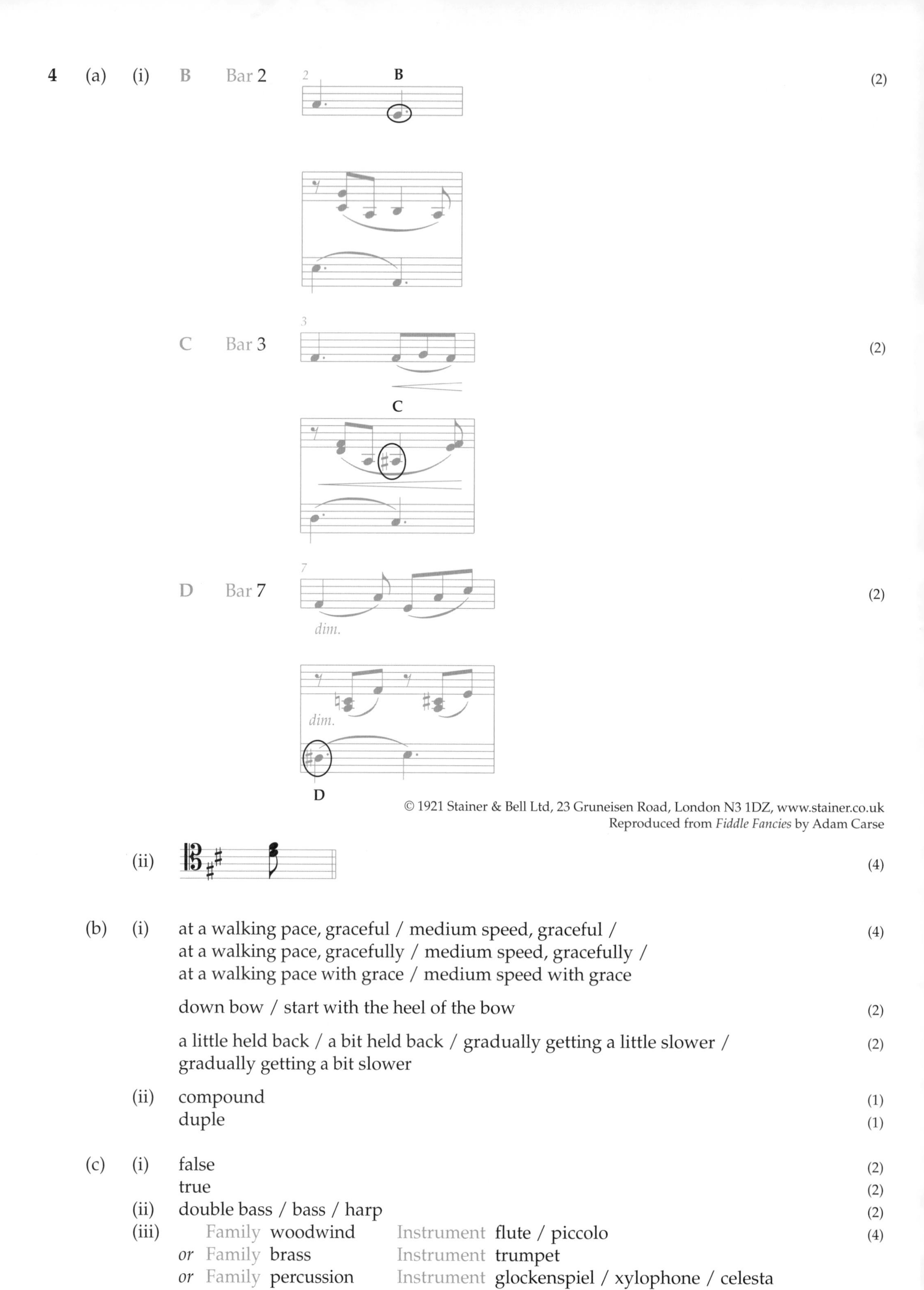

4 (a) (i) B Bar 2 (2)

C Bar 3 (2)

D Bar 7 (2)

(ii) (4)

(b) (i) at a walking pace, graceful / medium speed, graceful / at a walking pace, gracefully / medium speed, gracefully / at a walking pace with grace / medium speed with grace (4)

down bow / start with the heel of the bow (2)

a little held back / a bit held back / gradually getting a little slower / gradually getting a bit slower (2)

(ii) compound (1)
duple (1)

(c) (i) false (2)
true (2)

(ii) double bass / bass / harp (2)

(iii) Family woodwind Instrument flute / piccolo (4)
or Family brass Instrument trumpet
or Family percussion Instrument glockenspiel / xylophone / celesta

5 (10)

(a)

(b)

6 *There are many ways of completing this question. Either of the specimen completions below would receive full marks.* (15)

EITHER

(a) flute

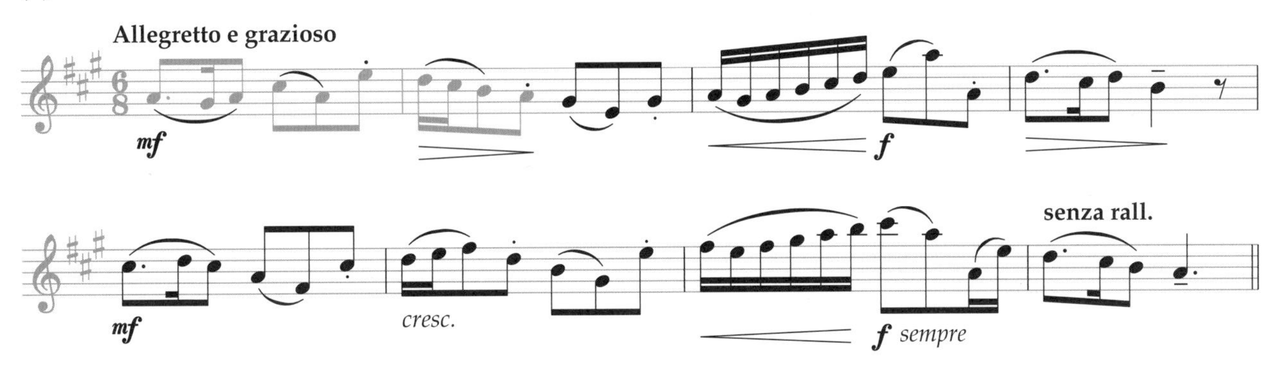

OR

(b)

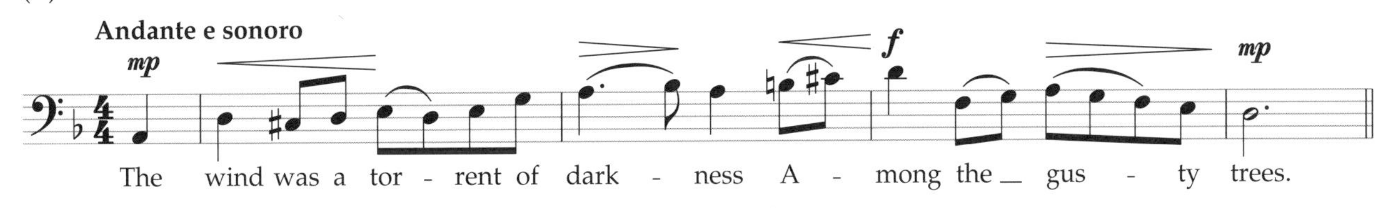

Text: Reproduced by kind permission of
The Society of Authors as the Literary Representative
of the Estate of Alfred Noyes

7 **EITHER** (10)

(a)

Chord A	II / G minor		Chord D	IV / B♭ major
Chord B	V / C major		Chord E	V / C major
Chord C	I / F major			

OR

(b)

A B C D E

Theory Paper Grade 5 2012 S
Model Answers

1 (a) Bar 1: $\frac{7}{8}$ Bar 2: $\frac{3}{8}$ Bar 3: $\frac{2}{4}$ / $\frac{4}{8}$ (6)

(b) (i) (2)

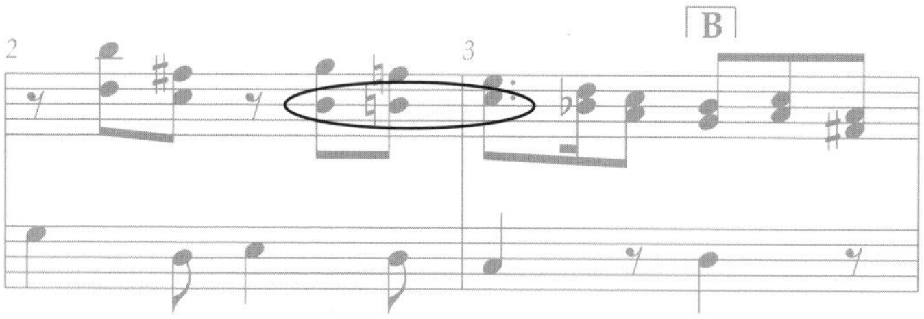

B

(ii) Chord **A** IV root / IVa (2)
Chord **B** I 5th / Ic (2)

(iii) (3)

2
1 augmented 4th (10)
2 minor 3rd
3 diminished 7th
4 perfect 12th / compound perfect 5th
5 minor 6th

3 (10)

Finzi, Fughetta (transposed)

4 (a) (i) *All possible answers are shown on the extract reproduced below.*
For full marks candidates need to identify only one example of each answer.

B Bar 6 (2)
C Bar 4 / 7 / 8 (2)

D Bar 3 (2)

(ii) Similarity rhythm / melodic shape / articulation / semiquaver rest (1)
Difference pitch / notes are a third lower in bar 6 / dynamics (1)

(iii) (2)

(b) (i) in the style of a march / march-like (2)
100 crotchets in a minute / 100 crotchet beats in a minute / (2)
100 quarter notes in a minute / 100 quarter-note beats in a minute

(ii) (4)

(iii) / / / / / (2)

(c) (i) true (2)
false (2)
false (2)

(ii) Instrument cello / double bass / bass / harp — Family strings (4)
or Instrument horn / trombone / bass trombone / tuba / bass tuba — Family brass

5

(10)

(a)

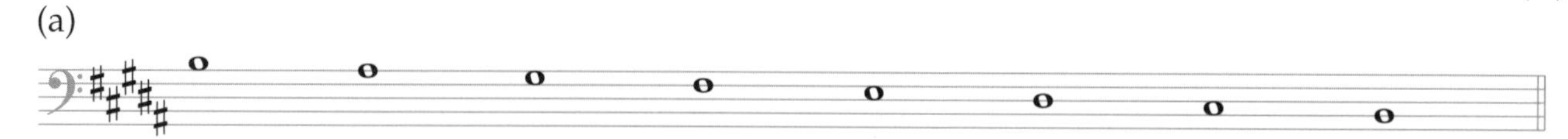

(b)

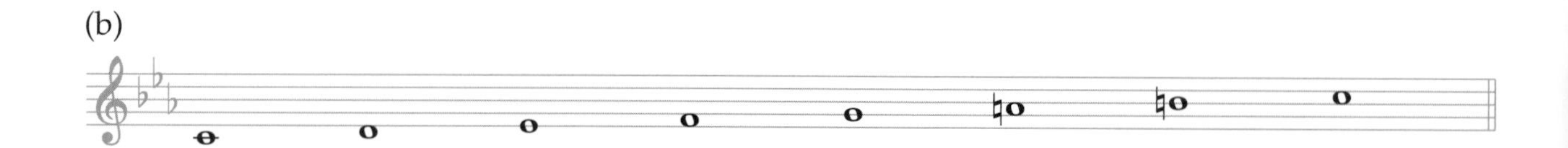

6 *There are many ways of completing this question. Either of the specimen completions below would receive full marks.* (15)

EITHER

(a) trombone

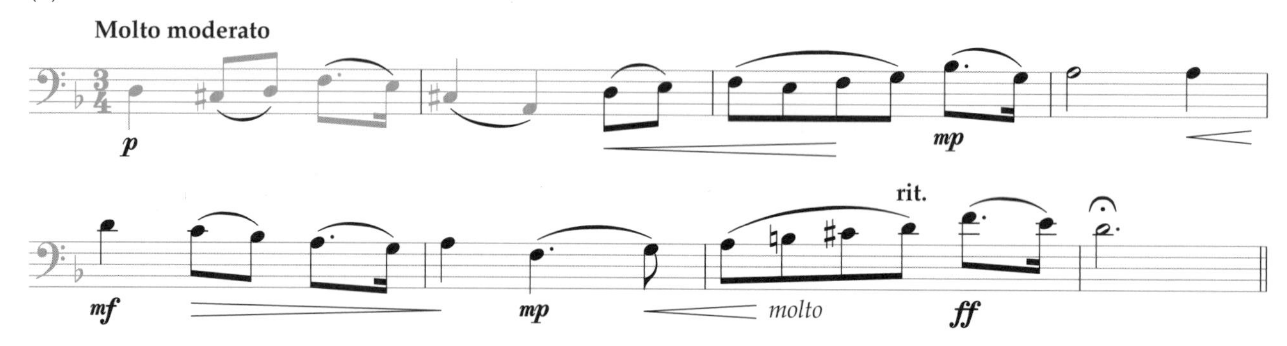

OR

(b)

7 **EITHER** (10)

(a) Chord A IV / C major
Chord B I / G major
Chord C II / A minor
Chord D V / D major
Chord E I / G major

OR

(b)

Music Theory Past Papers 2012 Model Answers

Model answers for four past papers from ABRSM's 2012 Theory exams for Grade 5

Key features:

- a list of correct answers where appropriate
- a selection of likely options where the answer can be expressed in a variety of ways
- a single exemplar where a composition-style answer is required

Support material for ABRSM Theory exams

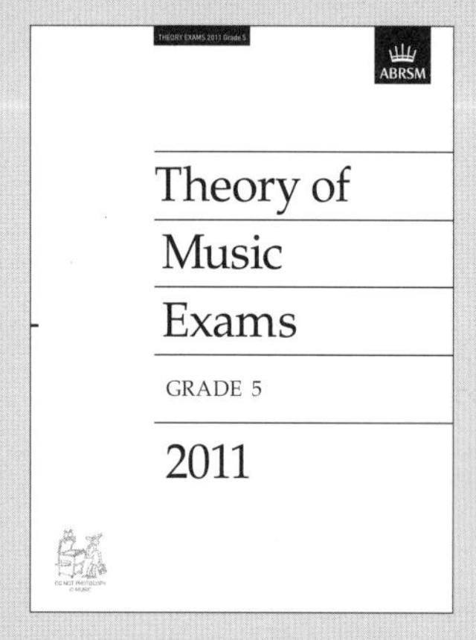

ABRSM
24 Portland Place
London W1B 1LU
United Kingdom

www.abrsm.org

ISBN 978-1-84849-468-8

ABRSM is the exam board of the Royal Schools of Music. We are committed to actively supporting high-quality music-making, learning and development throughout the world, and to producing the best possible resources for music teachers and students.